Forex Trading Made Easy For Beginners: Software, Strategies and Signals

The Complete Guide on Forex Trading Using Price Action

By: Marlon Green

PUBLISHERS NOTES

Disclaimer

This publication is intended to provide helpful and informative material. It is not intended to diagnose, treat, cure, or prevent any health problem or condition, nor is intended to replace the advice of a physician. No action should be taken solely on the contents of this book. Always consult your physician or qualified health-care professional on any matters regarding your health and before adopting any suggestions in this book or drawing inferences from it.

The author and publisher specifically disclaim all responsibility for any liability, loss or risk, personal or otherwise, which is incurred as a consequence, directly or indirectly, from the use or application of any contents of this book.

Any and all product names referenced within this book are the trademarks of their respective owners. None of these owners have sponsored, authorized, endorsed, or approved this book.

Always read all information provided by the manufacturers' product labels before using their products. The author and publisher are not responsible for claims made by manufacturers.

Paperback Edition

Manufactured in the United States of America

DEDICATION

This book is dedicated to my dad Nathaniel. He taught me how to trade and guided me through until now I am much more confident when I do it. He is all about family and has shown me by example how you have to do what you must to support your family.

Forex Trading Made Easy

TABLE OF CONTENTS

CHAPTER 1- A HISTORY OF FOREX

If you're like many people, you've probably heard the term "Forex" on the news or seen it in one of those ubiquitous, mildly-irksome banner ads found across the Internet, but you may have little detailed knowledge of this somewhat esoteric topic. The foreign exchange market, frequently referred to in truncated form as the "Forex market", "FOREX market", or "FX market", is, unbeknownst to many outside of finance, the largest financial market on the planet. Approximately four trillion U.S. dollars worth of currency is exchanged in this market every day, more value than that exchanged in the U.S. stock, bond, and T-bill markets combined.

Part of the reason the Forex market has limited visibility to those outside the world of finance is that, in contradistinction to other financial markets, the Forex market lacks a centralized exchange akin to the New York Stock Exchange (NYSE) or the Chicago Board Options Exchange (CBOE). The Forex market comprises a worldwide network of banks, other financial institutions, and independent Forex traders, all engaged in the trade of national and supranational currencies. A distinguishing trait of the Forex market is that it remains open and active 24 hours a day throughout the workweek, and since, as it were, the sun therefore never sets on the Forex market, it's also the most liquid of global markets.

In the past, access to the Forex market was only available to banks and other sizeable financial institutions, but as in so many other sectors, digital and information technology have leveled the playing field with respect to the Forex market. Forex trading is now readily available to all, from the traditional large players on down to money managers and individual traders. Accordingly, the past few years have seen many new traders enter this exciting, dynamic market. Getting started in Forex trading is now as simple as navigating to a Forex website and opening an account. Mastering Forex trading, however, is not necessarily any easier than it has ever been, as the market is still riddled with potential landmines for novices incognizant of their exposure to risk. Margined Forex trading, for example, is incredibly jeopardous and only appropriate for traders capable of absorbing the potential losses involved.

Because a brokerage account may offer the individual trader the capacity to trade currencies on a highly-leveraged basis, at values up to hundreds of times an account's underlying equity, this equity can potentially be entirely wiped out by swings in value of as small as a single percentage point, and the risk is only compounded in the current environment, wherein the euro and other major currencies have shown unusual volatility as a result of ongoing global macroeconomic uncertainties. Speculation in the Forex market should therefore only be exercised with "risk" capital, i.e., money that the investor can afford to lose.

Marlon Green

Trading foreign currencies in the Forex market is not at all similar to trading currencies in the futures market and is in many ways easier than trading stocks, commodities, and especially options. Indeed, practically all adults the world over are indirectly participating in the Forex market in a very real sense already. The simple possession of currency makes one an investor in that currency and affects its strength. The holding of renminbi, euros, or yen represents de facto decisions not to hold the currencies of other nations or regions.

Similarly, the purchase of equities and the holding of liquid cash in bank accounts or money-market mutual funds all point to faith in, or the fiat value of, the currencies in which those investments are denominated. Forex investing proper involves calculated gambles on how these and many other decisions by actors across the globe are likely to influence the relationships between different currencies. Changing currency values and the consequent fluctuations in exchange rates are the source of opportunity as well as risk in this market. As such, recent currency and thus exchange-rate volatility have led to considerable returns for Forex investors who have taken the right positions before and during, e.g., revolutions in the Arab world or anti-austerity riots in Europe.

To give an illustrative example, an investor with 20,000 pounds sterling (GBP) might trade all of these for Canadian dollars (CAD) when the exchange rate is 0.5 GBP to the CAD. He would then have 40,000 CAD. If the value of the CAD then increased against the GBP, as was the case in the years following the global economic downturn of 2008, he could then sell his CAD for GBP and end up with more pounds sterling than he had at the beginning.

Between these exchanges, our Forex trader would have kept track on a regular basis of exchange rates in the format "CAD/GBP last 0.653499", or something similar. This sample readout simply indicates that the last time an exchange between these currencies was recorded on the market; the rate was 0.653499 pounds sterling for a Canadian dollar. The first currency listed, here the CAD, is termed the "base" currency, and the second, the GBP, is called the "quote" or "counter" currency.

Forex trading is fundamental to the global economy as anyone who has ever exchanged currencies while traveling will be aware. So long as currencies continue to differ between countries (or at least regions), foreign currency exchange will be a prerequisite for the trade in products and services across those currency zones, and such international trade has only increased with advances in communication and transportation technology and as the infrastructure of globalization has continued to expand apace until the speculative eventuality of a unitary global.

CHAPTER 2- FOREX TRADING SYSTEMS

Looking for comprehensive and unbiased guides that will help you locate the best Forex trading system on the market? The information below will help you find the best Forex trading system that will bring you close to a system that will generate you profits and possibly a stable income stream in the least amount of time it takes to do so. A lot of individuals both employed and unemployed are utilizing Forex trading to support their financial necessities and help them in making ends meet.

Best Forex Trading System

A lot of individuals who venture off into the vast industry of foreign exchange market trading have no particular background in economics or finances whatsoever. This turns out to be a total waste of resources as the knowledge and skills required to work as a Forex trader is absent. This means that for any novice or beginning entrepreneur in Forex trading, one should first be versed about learning the ins and outs, tips and tricks and the facts about Forex trading before they can reach the coveted prize.

Even those who are experienced and have attained the appropriate credentials and educational background still make errors that are worth thousands of dollars. Imagine if you were only a novice who starts off without the slightest idea or knowledge regarding the matter. Though it is plausible, expect to mess up your trading accounts from the use of leverage and margin amounts.

As a newbie trader, learning how to intelligently trade Forex can be an overwhelming and daunting process, considering the voluminous information that one has to absorb combined with the continuously changing markets. In addition to these factors, scam artists and sharks are innumerable and are waiting to take advantage of novices who are looking for some sort of help and guidance. So for an aspiring yet uneducated and inexperienced trader, what is the best possible means of trading Forex wisely and lucratively?

One solution to learn how to trade Forex quickly and efficiently is to invest on the best Forex trading system. These software products will render you the basics of what you need to learn and master in order to quickly and profitably trade Forex. The best Forex trading system will also include tools and features that will allow you to hone your skills in Forex trading rather than just read bulky content and process the information by yourself.

So where do you find and purchase the best Forex trading system? Browsing the Internet, you'll find tons of options deeming themselves the "best Forex trading system." Though some may indeed be the best, it is imperative that you first research and study every possible option before you opt for any service provider of the best Forex trading system. This is to land on the most efficient and reliable product for your money as well as avoid risking your investments on scam products.

The first thing you will require when looking for the best Forex trading system is to have a sound knowledge of the basics of Forex trading and the Forex market. You need to understand and grasp the foundation of the concepts involved, such as the pips, leverage and the margin mean so that you can differentiate legitimate from illegitimate ones when you are offered with them. Moreover, you are required to know what you can risk and the values that are basically exposed on a good Forex trading system. For instance, it is possible to convert $100 into $10,000 with the use of large leverage and margin, yet the chances of doing so are lower when compared with betting and trading on a race track. This means when a trading system recommends utilizing bigger amounts for leverage during your initial investments, then this should alarm you that the system is potentially risky. The same concept applies for the "best Forex trading system" that promises to make you rich in just one night.

Then, you are required to understand the limitations and the basis of what makes the best Forex trading system the best. A continuously profitable trading system will be able to balance risk and profit. There are a few systems and automated software products in the market that display surprising returns and profits while having lower risks than other competing software products. Some of these software products claim to have winning rates of more than 90%. The truth of the matter is, even the best Forex trading system will show an equal share of loss and profit in the long run. This is why a lot of novices and beginning traders are immediately informed regarding the potential loss of their investments before they are taught to trade Forex.

Next, you will have to know the basics of technical and fundamental Forex analysis. Fundamental analysis relies upon the economic data and is basically identified by the economic and financial climate conditions as well as the economic data releases that are launched by different states and countries. Meanwhile, technical analysis is basically reliant upon the chart and the chart data. This particular field is more on mathematical orientation. Learning and mastering enough data regarding both areas is vital to profitably trade and to be able to identify what type of a trader you are.

Lastly, learn and master the trending indicators and confirmation. Your system should be able to inform you to search for a specified chart to identify whether the prices are moving up or down. The best Forex trading system can automatically do this responsibility for you. This process is vital as it determines if you can buy or sell the currency profitably. There are diverse indicators that you can use, such as support and resistance patterns, scalping and the most known and well recognized of all, the moving average crossover.

Overall, finding the best Forex trading system will enable you to make your ventures into the foreign exchange market easy and simple. One tip to remember when finding the best Forex trading system is to avoid hastily buying the product just because it is deemed as the best Forex trading system out there.

CHAPTER 3- FOREX TRADING PLATFORM

So which is the best Forex trading platform? Though it seems to be easy and simple to shop for Forex trading software due to the fact that you can find it virtually anywhere you go, the process is quite intricate and daunting at the same time since the myriad of choices laid out in front of you are innumerable and immensely varying. One error on your part may send you on the wrong path of your foreign exchange trading endeavors and prove to be a waste of valuable resources. So how do you go about undertaking this vital process?

Before tackling the how-to's, let's first discuss why you should consider investing on these products. The best Forex trading platform doesn't come free, and this is why some fail to realize the need for the software and disregard its value due to their perception of the product as being another monthly expense and financial liability on their part, an aspect that most novice traders cannot spare.

Forex Trading Made Easy

A major benefit of employing the best Forex trading platform from a reliable and competent service provider is that you can automate a lot of the common tasks and procedures that you normally would have to undertake and perform when investing on the Forex market online. Using the features and abilities of the best Forex trading platform, one is able to thoroughly check and identify the endlessly changing trends and the statistical analysis so that they will be able to come up with the best possible decision that will prove to be profitable for them. The best Forex trading platform also enables the user to bypass all the complexities involved in Forex trading and yields the capability of trading online in a simple and direct approach.

If you opt to invest in a do-it-yourself manner, the process of Forex trading is fairly redundant and, in some cases, confusing. This confusion and redundancy doubles for a novice and inexperienced trader. The best Forex trading platform will make the process much simpler, easier and centralized. Effortlessly log into your computer system, execute trading and investing tasks, check the recent transaction records and obtain valuable advice to base your final decision for buying or selling. This capability may prove to be highly useful and may yield the user with a powerful tool that they need in order to achieve a much greater profit value.

Accuracy is another advantage when using the best Forex trading platform. In the complicated and vast world of the foreign exchange market, all it takes to lose money directly from your pocket is a minor slip and a slight miscalculation of statistics. The power to check trends alongside personal history and then execute statistical analysis enables you to make a much more educated and more precise deliberation towards investing. With this, investors will be able to do more than simply making wild guesses and then hoping for something good in return.

Marlon Green

So how do you go about finding the best Forex trading platform and software that fits the bill? The first tip in looking for the best Forex trading platform is to ascertain that all indicators you are currently using in your trading strategies are all in the software product or, if not present, can be easily added. There may be nothing more disappointing than investing on a back testing software that is incapable of performing back tests due to the absence of one or multiple key indicators. The software product you utilize should have an extensive array of consistently utilized technical indicators. For the more known and recognized software bundles, you can typically obtain indicators by means of the Internet for free through visiting different Forex-related blog sites, forums and message boards.

Another essential component of the best Forex trading platform is a means for communication between both parties involved, the service provider and the client. If any issues or problems arise, the client should be able to pick up the phone or directly connect online with a customer support service representative to guide you in addressing the issue and provide a reliable and valuable solution. Usually, the means of communicating with the service provider's customer support department is through phone, email or by means of an integrated system that is displayed similar with a chat module within the system platform. This is imperative since all trading transactions are executed in real-time and when you require the specialized help, you should be able to get it in a few clicks or touch of the button.

Next, you should check if the best Forex trading platform is capable of giving you a clear and concise definition of a started and a starting trend. The best Forex trading systems start off trading with the starting trend as early as you confirm the emerging trends. Meanwhile, in the event that a trend has already been initiated, the software should be able to return to you the viable reversal points to it in order for you to make decisions against the trend as you may already be too late to catch up with the respective trend. Thus, keep in mind that the best Forex trading platform will render you both ends and possibilities of the trading transaction, both trading with and against the trend.

Aside from these factors and variables that are important to consider, there are also other crucial elements like trade profit-potential, win-loss ratios and draw-downs. A good foreign exchange trading system should be able to generate higher amounts of profit while minimizing the risk for loss to the least possible ratio. Preferably, the best Forex trading platform should have at least a 1:4 ratio for revenue potential and loss potential so that you know you're reaping more than what you are paying for monthly from using the service.

CHAPTER 4- FOREX TRADING STRATEGIES

Forex trading strategies or using a Forex trading strategy is one of the many ways to trade securities successfully. Trading is one of the most common activities to do in the financial securities sector. With trading you can buy and sell stocks, bonds, commodities and future. One of the other and more lucrative things you can trade is foreign exchanges. With foreign exchange trading you will be able to buy and sell currencies. By trading this type of security you can potentially have a very lucrative way to make money. While foreign exchange trading can be very lucrative you will need to adopt good Forex trading strategies in order to effectively and consistently make money with foreign exchange trading. By using good Forex trading strategies you will be able to make the most money possible and succeed.

Forex Trading Strategies

When it comes to Forex trading strategies and adopting a Forex trading strategy traders will need to use four main types of strategies. These strategies are basic, simple, complex and advanced. Over time traders will be able to advance and use all four Forex trading strategies over time. The first type of Forex trading strategy is the basic strategy. This is the beginner phase of trading and where the first education comes. With a basic Forex trading strategy traders will use simple charts and use basic pattern recognition in order to learn how the foreign exchange market works and how to effectively make profitable trades. It will also lead them to a better transition to the other more advanced phases of foreign exchange trading.

The next main Forex trading strategy is the simple Forex trading strategies. These strategies are known to be quite simple and rather easy to attempt. With the simple Forex trading strategies, traders will learn how to better research and develop various systems of trading. They will learn how to find workable trading techniques based on research and apply them to the current markets. When it comes to using simple foreign exchange trading strategies they are best used for traders who are either beginners of considerable skill or ones with intermediate experience.

However they are not really worth it for more advanced and experienced traders. For traders, it is very important to go through the simple strategy phase at it is critical to their development into becoming successful foreign exchange traders. The strategies learned will help them improve and have the ability to make profitable trades more often. So traders should not skip this step and take it lightly. This strategy is important for both short term and long term success in foreign exchange trading.

When it comes to foreign exchange trading, the next important step and Forex trading strategy is complex trading strategies. These strategies usually cover trading that is more complicated and advanced then the other two strategies. With complex trading, traders go into trading that contains more than three technical indicators of generating signals.

By using complex trading strategies, they will need to use many important rules in order to succeed with this type of strategy as well. By using the complex trading strategies, people will have the ability to explore new methods and develop more improved trading techniques in this type of securities trading. One thing that makes this strategy very good is its flexibility. Traders will be able to simplify systems to their preferences, apply certain rules and learn new things as they go along.

Marlon Green

The final Forex trading strategy that is necessary to use is the advanced strategy. In order to apply and use these strategies, traders will need to have a very good background in foreign exchange trading along with lots of theoretical knowledge. They will also have to be quite experienced and also know all of the techniques and rules that are present with foreign exchange trading. It is important to realize that all trading including this type consists of lots of risk so you will need to really know what you're doing. In this type of trading, you will also have occasional losses so you will need to keep this in mind. However with the advanced strategy you will be able to minimize the risk as well as the losses as you do this. Due to the knowledge and experience that traders have at this level, they will be able to be more disciplined and be patient when making trades. When using the advanced strategies traders will need to follow strict rules and never deviate from these rules.

Trading in the foreign exchange market is very much like all of the other types of trading markets. Traders will need to analyze the markets, figure out trends, go over key information regarding the economy and then make trades based on the probability of the security going up in value in the near future. As far as foreign exchange is concerned, traders will need to go over the value of the many currencies in the world. During the Forex trading process, they will need to go over economic trends, compare values between certain currencies and also make the trades if they believe that the value of one currency will rise soon. By using these strategies, traders in the foreign exchange market will have the necessary skills and knowledge to make good decisions and make trades that are profitable.

Whenever a person makes trades in the foreign exchange market they will need to learn and apply many things. As far as strategies are concerned they will need to use one level at a time. Those who are just starting will need to get the basic fundamental knowledge of the markets, trends, how to analyze securities, and also analyze the currencies. Once they get through this process they will then advance to the intermediate, complex and advanced strategies. Over time they will learn new things and new techniques to make profitable trades in the foreign exchange market. When it comes to strategies a combination of market analysis, knowledge, figuring out trends, determining probability are the best forms of a Forex trading strategy.

CHAPTER 5- FOREX SIGNALS

The best Forex signals play a significant role towards success for your Forex trading venture. However, it is quite intimidating and overwhelming to find which Forex signal system will work best for your specific needs and demands and which one is just a hoax. There are countless options that deem themselves as the best Forex signals on the current market. Nonetheless, it is important that you don't get lost in the process of shopping for the best Forex signals from alluring ads and generous offerings that you come by when browsing for companies and service providers.

So how do you go about finding the best Forex signals you can possibly use? There are certain variables worth considering prior to investing on the best Forex signals. These variables contribute to good trading signal software and adhering within these factors and making them your parameters in which to base the final decision will enable you to land on the most suitable trading signal for your individual needs. Here are some of the factors you should keep in mind when shopping for the best Forex signals. Finding the best Forex trading signals service provider isn't rocket science, however, one should still keep in mind some things before choosing the most reliable and competent service provider to employ.

First, a good Forex trading signal service provider should be able to simplify the process of foreign exchange trading. It is no secret that the industry of Forex trading has several complexities that even the most skilled and experienced traders manage to fall into. This means that the complexities and issues may aggregate when tackled by a novice trader. And in order to reach the goldmine that everyone aims in achieving during Forex trading, these complexities must be solved and the challenges must be surpassed. With the software's help, you should be able to bypass all the responsibilities, such as keeping track on the movement and alterations of the foreign exchange market, and make the process automated by using the Forex trading signal software.

Second, review the recurring costs charged by the service provider. The best Forex signals should charge reasonable and affordable monthly fees. Before considering the options laid out on the table, you should estimate the potential profits you can make and calculate the monthly fees that you are charged with. Most service providers will charge a fee that can amount up to $100. If you manage to get this amount of fee for your monthly premiums, you should aim to make revenues that are greater than the fee to compensate for the monthly charges. If you are unable to do so, this means that you are spending more than you are gaining from using the Forex trading signal system.

Next, avoid depending on contents that you read on forums for your final decision. Though forums are no doubt a good and reliable source of data, they also contain data that are biased against a particular company. Forums and message boards may sometimes be where companies pull advertisement stunts to gain exposure for free. You will find a lot of positives and negatives that are mentioned in a particular service.

Though the negatives are there, it still does not prove the legality of the software product or if it's one of the best Forex signals out there. It is best to avoid getting information and basing your final decision from forums when shopping for the best Forex trading signal. Instead, you should research company information or data from the developer of the software online.

Fourth, consider risk and money management. A lot of the best Forex signals service provider renders clients great value information regarding profits and stop-loss. Although there is no need to pay attention to information, you will have to focus on the part of proper money management. Having the right skill set and knowledge base regarding your budget and how to spend it intelligently will prevent you from incurring heavier losses. Moreover, you may incur heavy consequences when you seek help and guidance from a service provider that is extremely unreliable. Thus, make sure that it is something which you can bank on as you progress on to your Forex trading venture.

Fifth, test the service. Trying out each and every trading system is a vital component of trading, and with signals, it is no different. You can simply test out the best Forex signals by means of employing a dummy account and then evaluating it as early as possible. Although it will take up some time and money from your wallet, it is actually worth the investments you put into it.

The sixth tip in finding the best Forex signals is to track records. Browsing the Internet, you will find countless advertisements for trading signal service providers. A scam artist can effortlessly lure in traders with alluring and seemingly realistic advertisements and nearly impossible promises, such as higher yields and even overnight accumulation of profit. It is sometimes complex to identify which provider is legit and which is not. You can find a variety of comparison tools that you can use for free online as well as lists and databases of the best Forex signals service providers that rank them in accordance to the company's average pips.

Lastly, choose the best Forex signals that offer a free trial period. No matter how great and valuable the information and records you manage to find and amass from hours of research, this information is unmatched when you manage to personally test out the software for a given period of time. Free trial options will render a hands-on experience and will give you a clearer insight and feel on the system that you are about to buy.

The best Forex signals service providers should also have different features and capabilities that can comply with a professional Forex trader and at the same time offer an easy, simple yet still efficient platform for novice traders. Overall, make sure to invest both time and effort for looking for the best Forex signals out there in order to improve your chances of success in the Forex trading industry.

CHAPTER 6- WHAT TO TRADE IN FOREX

So, what do the people trade? On other exchanges, speculators trade for a piece of ownership in a certain product or business. The Forex market is a little bit different, in that they are trading actual currencies. Some of the more popular ones include:

- EUR/USD
- GBP/JPY
- USD/CAD

These currencies are put together in what is called pairs. Newcomers to Forex learn trading these pairs above more often than not. A good way to think of it for those that want to learn Forex trading is to imagine someone going away on vacation to a foreign country. When the person arrives in that country, they will need to exchange their currency for the new country's currency. A week later they are ready to return home. The value of their home currency has gone up in comparison to the foreign country's currency. What this means, is that they will now hand over their vacation money in exchange for their home currency at less value since their home currency went up. This means a loss in value. On the other hand, if the country they are visiting has an increased value of their currency, the vacationer stands to make money on the transaction.

How It Is Traded

In some aspects, it is similar to that of any other stock market. There is a buying price, and a selling price. This is represented in a bid/ask equation. The bid is the price someone is willing to pay for a particular currency pair. The ask price is what someone wants to sell their currency at in hopes of gaining a profit when they buy it back. This is often the most difficult part for people to understand when they learn Forex trading.

How to Predict Movement

Beginners to Forex learn trading in roughly 2 basic, but different areas. The first is considered to be fundamental analysis. The second is technical analysis. Many arguments have been placed over which one is the most accurate. Some people have great success just with technical indicators, while others only look at nonfarm payroll reports to predict what their currency market will do. In short, they're both right. It's important that new speculators to Forex learn trading in both these areas of market analysis.

Fundamental analysis takes on a broad scope of factors to pinpoint down what the currency will do. Some traders look for trends in GDP of the two countries they are comparing. Another type of fundamental analysis can include news headlines. It's amazing what bad news and good news alike can do to a currency within a short amount of time.

The other style, for those looking to learn Forex trading, is technical analysis. This is primarily done just by reading charts and noticing trends. This also takes a lot of grit and determination. The charts are compared to historical data, and this data has a long history. However, those that can decipher these charts will see clear patterns emerge.

Types of Traders

There are also different styles, that those new to Forex learn trading. For casual or more conservative types of speculators, they are usually drawn to swing trading and trend trading. Trend trading is probably the most conservative of all styles. In other stock markets, it's also referred to as buy-and-hold. Here the speculator feels a trend may not reach its true potential for six months to a year, or even longer down the road. Swing trading is kind of a middle-of-the-road style. These types of trades can last anywhere from one day to a month. This type of speculator likes to play it safe, but still wants a degree of interaction.

A third style of trader is the day trader. This speculator likes to live life in the fast Lane. Their trades can last a few minutes to a couple hours, but generally their positions will be finished by the end of the day. There is even a kind of sub category to the day traders. These are called scalpers. Scalpers can sit on a position for just mere seconds while trying to catch a momentary upswing for profit. This is highly interactive, and can be dangerous to a person who has just started to learn Forex trading. Newcomers to Forex learn trading in one of these fashions, and usually decide quickly which is more their speed.

Forex is an exciting world, which can also be a rewarding one to those who put in the effort. Make no mistake about it though; there is a huge learning curve. For those that want to learn Forex trading, they have a long road ahead of them, if they wish to see the real beauty of leverage.

CHAPTER 7- MORE ABOUT AUTOMATED FOREX TRADING

If you want to start trading on the Forex market, you may not know where to begin, but automated Forex trading software can make the process much easier than a person might imagine. A user still needs to learn the basics of Forex trading and have a good idea of what the market is like. If he does not know what the market is like, he may not know what he is getting into. If he does not know what he is getting into he can lose a lot of the money he is attempting to investment. Financial investing always involves risks. The user wants to minimize the risk while maximizing his gains. Any investing book can tell a user that much, what the user needs to know is how he can gain an advantage.

Automated Forex Trading Software

Marlon Green

There are many different systems that purport to tell someone how to trade with foreign currency. The systems all work with the same basic premise, although each book may offer its own strategies. Automated Forex trading software testimonials may or may not mention automated Forex trading software. It is unlikely that the systems will work as well as some of the system's author's claim. A reader can take away useful strategies from many of these self-proclaimed experts. The automated Forex trading software package just takes a lot of the work out of the process.

When someone looks for a good automated Forex trading software package, he needs to know how it works, which networks it connects to, and how often it checks the Internet. The best Forex automated software packages will check with the Internet periodically. The user wants to make sure the reports are updated in real-time. Foreign currencies are traded against each other all the time. Because currencies are traded against each other all the time, the prices fluctuate. Trends are still traced over days, but an automated system can help a person buy and sell at opportune moments. A person may find that he can make a large profit during the course of a single day using automated Forex trading software. It is unlikely that this will happen over the course of a single day, but modern information technology makes this a possibility.

Automated Forex trading software can be desktop based or web based. The web based software can be accessed from a browser, although the desktop client software can store far more information. The extra information lets a user track the performance. The more advanced automated Forex trading software web packages can do this for you. Automated Forex trading software usually needs to be connected to a computer with Internet access that is on all the time.

This is true whether it is attached to a web server or if it is attached to a person's home computer. Even if it is attached to a person's home computer, it still needs to access the server that contains the required information. When a user understands that he needs an Internet connection that is active almost all of the time, he can decide on an automated Forex trading package that will meet his or her needs.

Linux users may not be able to find an automated Forex trading software package that works with their computer. There may be one or two commercial packages that will serve this purpose. Open source investors may have provided a package for his fellow Linux and UNIX enthusiasts. Users of WINE may be able to get such a package to run under his favorite Linux distribution. A user of Windows or the Apple operating system has things much easier. Commercial developers do not shy away from support of these operating systems. Linux users do not have a lot of automated Forex trading software options.

There will be hundreds of desktop automated trading software commercial packages that can be sold for varying prices to the user. The price of each automated Forex trading software package depends on its intended target market. Some packages are designed only to be run on servers. The server packages often are designed to be plugged into browser and are written in Active Server Pages, Ajax, JavaScript and other web scripting languages. The software will have to find a way to store the data for each user. Fortunately, this is a problem of the programmer has to solve. The user does not need to worry about it.

The best software packages should be easy to set up and have a small learning curve. The small learning curve is necessary as investing itself has a large learning curve. Some people enjoy working with technology and plying the financial markets, but most people choose one or the other. If a person chooses to learn investing but does not have time to follow the markets the way that he should, he may find that an automated Forex trading software package can free his time for other activities. He can even learn how to do other types of investing. Financial experts recommend that people diversify their portfolio, after all.

Automated trading software has another advantage. The software can help someone who does not know the ins and outs of investing. Automated Forex software can help keep someone on the safer track of investing, although no investment is perfectly safe. Even someone who puts his money in a bank is betting that the bank will not collapse. Larger financial markets carry even more risk than a savings account or a certificate of deposit.

Although a person can gain many benefits from using such a package, he should know that there are limitations. One of the most severe limitations of automated Forex trading software occurs because it relies on electrical equipment. Electrical equipment can fail. If a computer goes out during a trading process, the user can fail to make an important trade. It can also prevent a trade that can lose money. Every electrical and electronic device shares this weakness. Software may not be a device, but it relies on electronic devices to run correctly. As long as the user knows what he is getting into, he can proceed with confidence. Automated Forex trading software can give a user confidence, but it does not always let the brilliance of an investor shine through.

ABOUT THE AUTHOR

Marlon Green is a much more confident trader than he was initially thanks to his dad. He does it part time for now but has plans one day to do it full time as he would be able to do it from home and be closer to his family. He did a lot of research and from all the information that he gathered he was able to write an introductory guide of his own to help others to learn about the basics of Forex trading.

His main aim with his books is to inform and educate and he finds that persons are extremely receptive as long as the information can be easily understood.